IMAGES
of America

MATAMORAS
TO SHOHOLA
A JOURNEY THROUGH TIME

PIKE COUNTY, PENNSYLVANIA.

—‡—

Has become noted the country over as a summer resort, ranking next to any section on the American continent. It is within 100 miles of Greater New York and Philadelphia, is easy of access and any part of its domain can be reached from either city in from three to twenty-four hours. The Delaware River bounds it for about 60 miles, the Wallenpaupack is on the north boundary and mountains surround the remainder. The scenery in this county is equal to any on this continent or Europe. Its magnificent waterfalls, romantic glens, fine roads and drives, picturesque walks, excellent facilities for boating, bathing, fishing and hunting and the purity and abundance of its springs and mountain streams, the health-giving influence of its invigorating air, commend this county to the tourist in spring, summer or autumn. There are more lakes in Pike than any other county in the state.

A PIKE COUNTY LAKE.

NEXT RACES will be held on Saturday, September 14th, 1901, at 2 p. m.

BASE BALL, Monday, Sept. 2d, 1901, 3.30 p. m. See announcement inside.

SECTION OF A MILFORD STREET.

.... MILFORD ....

—‡—

This beautiful village is located on the bank of the Delaware River and commands an extended view of the Delaware Valley and Blue Mountains of New Jersey. It has one of the most noted water supplies in the country and malaria and mosquitoes are almost unknown. It is but 7 miles from a railroad. Milford boasts a bank, water company, gas company, telephone company, telegraph, long distance telephone, two newspapers, hotels, boarding houses, stores, two drug stores, third class post office with eight mails a day, three barber shops, several laundries, six livery stables, three lodges, butchers, bakers, blacksmiths, shoe dealers, painters, lumber dealers, contractors, two mills, and numerous other smaller

This is an advertisement from 1901. (Courtesy of Jayne Schroeder Manzer.)

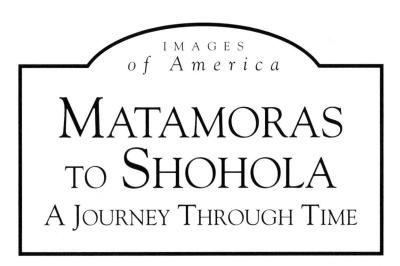

IMAGES
of America

MATAMORAS TO SHOHOLA
A JOURNEY THROUGH TIME

Matthew M. Osterberg

ARCADIA

First printed in 1998.
Reprinted in 2002.

Published by Arcadia Publishing,
an imprint of Tempus Publishing, Inc.
2A Cumberland Street
Charleston, SC 29401

Printed in Great Britain.

For all general information contact Arcadia Publishing at:
Telephone 843-853-2070
Fax 843-853-0044
E-Mail sales@arcadiapublishing.com

For customer service and orders:
Toll-Free 1-888-313-2665

Visit us on the internet at http://www.arcadiapublishing.com

*This book is dedicated to my wife, Carol,
and my children, Stephanie and Michael.*

CONTENTS

ACKNOWLEDGMENTS

There are many people and organizations to thank for helping in the preparation of this book. I would like to begin by thanking my wife, Carol, and Lizanne Samuelson who helped me tremendously in captioning photographs and keeping me on course. Without their help, I would not have completed this endeavor. Sandy Leiser also spent hours captioning photographs and for that I am very grateful. The Pike County and Minisink Valley Historical Societies and the Millrift Civic Association who opened their vast collections of photographs for my use are also deserving of my thanks. Specifically, I would like to thank Steve Szabara, Bob Longcore, Peter Osborne, and Karen Gropman for helping locate photographs at these societies and Bill Clark, the Matamoras historian, for his complete support.

The following individuals were generous in sharing their personal photographs and memories that helped in creating this book: Centa Quinn, Merritt Quinn, Marc Sorbe, Mr. and Mrs. Richard Basham, Margaret Fuller, Monk Rake, Fred Herbst, Mr. and Mrs. Albert Luhrs, Mr. and Mrs. Edward Hess, Mr. and Mrs. Joe Herbert, Ethel Musselwhite, Sonny Calestini, Gladys Raymond, Iona and Bob Blood, Dick Gassmann, James May, Mr. and Mrs. Richard Lutfy, Mrs. Ted Buchanan, the people of St. Patrick's Church and the people of St. Joseph's Church, Betty Lou Dugan, Jayne Schroeder Manzer, Red Helms, Dennis Gilpin, George Fluhr, Carol and Gene Husson, Carl Mulhauser, Kitty Myer, Joanna McGaughey, Christine Richards, Donald Hinkel Jr., Tom Hoff, Leith Hoffman, William Schneider, Fred DeGroat and the members of the Matamoras Fire Department, Mr. and Mrs. William Fleming, Barbara Orben, Richard Snyder, Howard Brunhoelzl, Donald Gerola, James Bianchi, Matamoras Alumni Association, Mr. and Mrs. Raymond Orben, Mr. and Mrs. Richard Brown, Jim Crawford, John Misenhelder, Bill Kiger, Valerie Meyer, Wendy Steuber, Andrew Monisera, Beth Lovett, Mr. and Mrs. Harry Buchanan, Allan Berner, Skip and Lorraine Gregory, and the folks at the Pike County Library. A special thank you to the individuals who wrote so extensively on this area of Pike County. These resources were invaluable in writing the captions for the photographs: *Mathew's History of Monroe, Wayne and Pike Counties, Pennsylvania 1886*, by Alfred Mathews; William Henn's *Westfall Book*; George Fluhr's many publications; Norman Lehde and Sandy Leiser's books, *Pike County* and *Milford's 250th Anniversary*; *Crossroads*—a book on Milford's architecture by the Pike County Historic Project in 1980; and Matthew Gatzke's research paper.

INTRODUCTION

Matamoras to Shohola: A Journey Through Time is a photographic history, depicting life from 1860 to 1960 in six of the 13 Pike County rural communities: Westfall (Millrift), Milford Township, Milford Borough, Dingman Township, Shohola (Pond Eddy), and Matamoras, whose ancestors settled the ancient and glacial Minisink Valley in the early 1700s. For eons of geological time, the beautiful Delaware River, which forms a natural border between Pennsylvania, New York, and New Jersey, has continued to touch the shores along Matamoras to Shohola and has effected the culture and economy of its proud residents.

The bountiful Delaware River fertilized the lowlands for farming and allowed the commercial transportation of timber and bluestone for the buildings and sidewalks of many major cities. The railroad brought visitors from New York City and Philadelphia to the grand hotels and comfortable boardinghouses situated along the tranquil streams and scenic foothills of the Pocono Mountains in Northeastern Pennsylvania.

Tourists arrived by train via Port Jervis, New York, and Pond Eddy/Shohola, Pennsylvania, and were picked up by stagecoaches and transported to their "tourist destinations." Although the Great Depression closed the doors of many popular boardinghouses and luxurious hotels, the prosperity occurring at the close of World War I and World War II encouraged urban families to build summer cottages and permanent homes in Pike County.

Looking at old photographs to see how some things have changed and how other things have stayed the same thrilled me. Time and trends alter certain architectural features, but, fortunately, a considerable number of old buildings remain standing (Jay's Handy Corner in Matamoras and the Emily Cottage in Milford), while tragically many exist no more (Indian Point in Dingman Township and the original Evergreen Lodge in Westfall). It is essential that the history of any community is preserved, and one way to accomplish this important goal is to show people how a community lived in the past. *Matamoras to Shohola: A Journey Through Time* is a part of this commitment to historical preservation and the enhancement of an economy dependent on tourism.

This book's presentation of rare photographs provides a vision of life in small communities when the world was a larger place in which to live and people moved at a slower pace.

Turn these historic pages and learn how a few communities developed in a little corner of one of the original colonies and came to play a significant role in America as it emerged from 1860 to 1960 to become the greatest power in the world. Enjoy pictures of magnificent homesteads, busy farms, cascading waterfalls, enterprising merchants, and famous people, and realize the enduring contributions made by the Dutch, German, and French immigrants.

While Pike County has a rich heritage of historical landmarks and natural resources, it is people and organizations that have made these communities special. Photographs of early schoolhouses (Quicktown School in Westfall and the Matamoras High School), country churches (St. Jacobi's Lutheran Church in Shohola and St. John's Episcopal Church in Milford), festive parades (Milford's Fourth of July Firemen's Parade), and civic groups (Matamoras's Christmas Basket) give us a clear understanding of how vital educational, religious, and civic responsibility have always been in these close communities.

As these interesting pages are turned, the reader will see how Matamoras to Shohola is a unique region comprised of wonderful neighborhoods, each distinctly representing the era of its growth (the De Behrle Cottage in Milford and children playing on a pony cart in Westfall). This journey through time takes us back to the past but in many photographs confirms the present. I was successful in gathering photographs of hotels and restaurants still in operation (Rohmans in Shohola and the Dimmick Inn in Milford), as well as changing street and water views.

In this book, I will tell the story of one hundred years of intense economic transformations, beginning with the horse and carriage deliveries (horse and buggy on Raymondskill) and moving toward the surrender of the railroad (Pond Eddy train station) and the invention of the automobile (cruising down Broad Street). I'll conclude with a helicopter bringing Pres. John F. Kennedy to Milford Township (landing at Grey Towers) as Matamoras to Shohola grew and America came to lead the world.

Hopefully, this book will visually inspire the thoughtful reader with a lasting awareness that all communities must preserve their history in order to ensure the future. The next time you decide to discard your old photographs and memorabilia, contact the author by mail at 107 East High Street, Milford, Pennsylvania 18337. Who knows, your photographs might just be the reason for another "journey through time."

Matthew M. Osterberg
June 1998

One

TOURISM

Some years after serving in the Civil War, John H. McCarty, whose grandfather had been a soldier in the Revolutionary War, returned to the Raymondskill Falls area in Dingman Township. He became the owner of the falls and surrounding land and lived in the Raymondskill Falls House located near the falls c. 1879. Subsequently his grandson, Beraldi McCarty, built the Indian Point Inn overlooking the Delaware. The property was owned by five generations of McCartys until it was purchased by the Army Corp. of Engineers in the 1970s at which point the inn was destroyed. (Collection of the Pike County Historical Society.)

The Conashaugh Spring House of Dingman Township offered one hundred rooms for 175 guests in its prime *c.* 1870. Its brochure proclaimed "select patronage with references available as far south as Savannah, Georgia." No spirits were served, and the hotel was destroyed by fire in 1915. (Collection of the Pike County Historical Society.)

The Shanna House was a well-patronized establishment along the River Road (Route 209). After the Park Service bought it, the Splendora family operated it for many years as a fine restaurant. It burned not long ago, but the "garage" seen in this 1920s picture is still standing near the intersection of Route 209 and the Raymondskill Road. (Collection of the Pike County Historical Society.)

The Hotel Schanno, located in Dingman Township off Route 1, was built by the sons of Emile Schanno, who had come to this country in the early 1800s after he lost his property in his native Alsae during the Franco-Prussian War. The hotel became the favorite rendezvous of the elite coach trade and earned the nickname "Little Delmonico" after the famous New York City eatery because of the excellence of its cuisine. In recent years, it was the "Red Fox" and the "Bistro Primavera." It was recently razed to make way for the new Milford Bible Church. (Courtesy of the Quinn Family.)

The original part of the Arlington Hotel was built by Frank Seitz in the late 1880s for his parents. The Seitzes ran the business until Frank lost the hotel in a card game to Mr. Thorton, whose family owned the Dimmick Inn. The expansion of the building took place over the years by subsequent owners. In the 1980s the burned-out remains of the hotel were demolished and the American Legion Post #139 built their present structure on the site. (Collection of the Pike County Historical Society.)

This is a view of Golden Spring House in Dingman Township *c.* 1911. (Collection of the Pike County Historical Society.)

This is a photograph of the Cliff Park Inn in Dingman Township taken *c.* 1910. Originally the Buchanan (Bowhannon) Farmhouse, it was built around 1820 near the high and scenic cliffs overlooking the Delaware River. In 1900, Harry and Anne Buchanan transformed it into a spacious and elegant boardinghouse, and later, family members converted the field into a large and popular golf course which visitors continue to enjoy today. This estate has been in the Buchanan family since 1803. (Courtesy of Harry Buchanan.)

20406

Pocono Farm, built in 1866 by James C. Rose, was located on 250 prime acres along the Delaware in Westfall Township. It was a favorite resort in the days of stage travel conveniently situated on the main stage road. Plagued by fire in the early 1900s, it was further devastated by the flood of 1903, which the *Milford Dispatch* described as follows: "The water came into the first floor of Rose's Pocono Farm House and his woodpile and several hundred bushels of apples were scattered along the roadway for some distance." Beset again in 1924 by a fire that leveled the structure, many thought the resort was gone for good but it was rebuilt and used as a dormitory, among other things, for the flying cadets training at the Matamoras Airport. In later years, it was operated by the Masurack family until it was sold. It is now home to the Golden Acres Retirement Home. (Courtesy of the Hinkel family.)

The original Evergreen Lodge was one of the two "halfway houses" located on the old Port Jervis-Milford Road. Its many patrons will remember the large mural behind the bar depicting native wildlife. It was razed and buried in the construction of Route 84. (Courtesy of Howard Brunhoelzl.)

S.D. Wells Crystal Spring Farm on the Parker's Glen Road could accommodate 15 guests per week and provided free conveyance from the railroad station 2 miles away. In 1906, the cost per guest per week was $6, but children under 12 could stay for half price. For many years it was operated by the Hinkel family and boasted a nine-hole golf course. Today it is a private residence. (Courtesy of the Hinkel family.)

Camp Sagamore was located where Sagamore Estates is now off of Route 6 West in Shohola Township. The camp was established in the 1930s by Edward, Burt, and Brick Lloyd as an adult summer resort. Men and women had separate cabins, but came together for recreational fun such as playing tennis, square dancing, or dining at the buffet suppers. Four hundred people could be accommodated and many availed themselves of water sports on Twin Lakes. This is the Twin Lakes Road entrance in the 1930s. (Courtesy of Gene and Carol Husson.)

This is a picture postcard taken in the early 1940s of Camp Shawnee overlooking Little Twin Lakes in Shohola Township. Camp Shawnee was for boys only and it was established in 1921 by Samuel D. Perry. About one hundred boys ages six to 16 years old enjoyed swimming, horseback riding, boating, and basketball. (Courtesy of Tom Hoff.)

15

In 1906, Pine Mountain Cottage in Parker's Glen, Shohola, was operated by George Burgard and could house 25 guests a week at $5 per week. Children were charged according to their age but servants cost $5 per week. The cottage offered a free bathroom but charged 50¢ for conveyance from the railroad station. (Courtesy of the Hinkel family.)

The Delaware View Farm in Parkers Glen was operated by Nicholas Shields. This three-story farm accommodated 40 guests. The Eberz family currently owns the property. (Courtesy of the Hinkel family.)

In 1912, Parker's Glen was the home to many boardinghouses, including Frank Keller's Delaware Mountain House. Many of these homes were destroyed in the Flood of 1955. (Courtesy of the Hinkel family.)

As seen in this 1910 postcard, Peter Eckhart kept the Oak Grove Cottage. It was located on German Hill Road in Shohola Township. Today the property is owned by Mickey Lauer. (Courtesy of the Hinkel family.)

The Rockview Manor in Shohola was a popular boardinghouse located near German Hill and was in operation until the 1940s. (Courtesy of Andrew Monisera.)

Not all of the early German settlers, most of them coming from the Hesse-Darmstadt area of Germany, were proponents of the temperance movement, and the thriving German Hotel provided them with fine beer. The hotel is still standing near the end of Glen Drive in Shohola and is privately owned. (Collection of the Pike County Historical Society.)

The Watson House, built in the late 1800s, was a very popular resort and boardinghouse on the smaller Twin Lake. Gifford Pinchot and Lionel Barrymore were among its many renowned guests. The house also served as a popular nightspot for campers at nearby Camp Sagamore. The building was razed in 1969 and the property is now privately owned. (Collection of the Pike County Historical Society.)

The Parkers Glen Fountain by Moonlight, Pike Co., Pa.

The Parkers Glen Fountain was accidentally created by the Erie Railroad when they wanted to establish a railroad stop at Parkers Glen village. They put a strainer in a long pipe at the base of the Walker Lake Falls and ran the pipe under the railroad track to ensure the tracks would be safe from running water. The gravitational force of the water created the fountain, which was a wondrous sight to behold on the Delaware River until the fountain was washed out by Hurricane Diane in 1955. (Courtesy of the Hinkel family.)

Rohman's Hotel
Shohola, Pa.

Rohman's Hotel in Shohola was built by Frank A. Kilgour in the late 1800s and was called the Shohola Glen Hotel. In his day, spirits were not sold, as in fact there existed "The Frank A. Kilgour Total Abstinence Society." In 1886, the hotel was described as having superior facilities that afforded the pleasure-seekers a skating rink and a place to dance, and it was considered "a wonderful place for busy men during their summer vacation." Arthur Rohman operated the inn from 1901 to 1973, when former Pike County Commissioner James Duffy took over the popular establishment.

Today visitors can enjoy the historic atmosphere of Rohman's and page through the old guest register, which includes such renowned signatures as those of Charles Lindbergh, Paul Newman, Lionel Barrymore, and Mary Pickford. Rohmans is listed on the National Historic Register and is presently owned by Sheila Farrell and Martin and Virginia Sheridan. (Courtesy of Andrew Monisera.)

Norman Coykendall, a Milford "character," was known locally as the "human fish." He owned a home, pool, and beach on the Delaware River near the present-day Milford Beach. He loved to have people tie him to a chair and throw him into the river from which he would emerge carrying the chair. (Courtesy of Fred Herbst.)

This is a 1940s postcard of the Coykendall's swimming pool along the Delaware River in Milford. (Courtesy of Mr. and Mrs. William Fleming.)

The Bluff House was built in 1876 by H.G. Wells. It was situated on the bluff of what is now 312 East Ann Street, Milford. Later proprietors of the Bluff House were Paul and Kitty Bournique, and ultimately three additions allowed for the accommodation of 350 guests, including servants. The Bluff House had everything: hot and cold running water, steam radiator heat, private baths, and a laundry room. Wealthy urban families would come for the season and enjoy large parlors, a children's playroom, a billiard room, and a bowling alley. There was entertainment every evening in the form of dances and concerts, and all visitors enjoyed the rocking chairs on the large verandahs overlooking the Delaware River. Water sports abounded, and the hotel was enjoyed by thousands until it burned in 1947. (Courtesy of the Hinkel family.)

Bob Blood began operating his river resort, known as "Bob's Beach," in Dingman Township in 1935. It was a popular meeting place enjoyed by residents and tourists. In the early 1970s, the property along the Delaware River was purchased by the National Park Service. (Courtesy of Bob Blood.)

The Laurel Villa Lodge is one of five buildings that make up the Laurel Villa complex that covers ten borough lots on the eastern border of Milford. Owned over the years by several families, it was under the management of the Doscher and Mulhauser families when modern conveniences were added. It was the first place in Milford to install air conditioning and has been patronized by local folks as well as tourists since its inception. The lodge is still open to the public, but the much-enjoyed public pool has been closed for a number of years. (Courtesy of Carl Mulhauser.)

This photograph, taken in the 1950s, depicts the sitting room of the Laurel Villa in Milford. People longed to escape the hustle and bustle of the city and enjoyed their time spent in the elegant Laurel Villa. (Courtesy of Carl Mulhauser.)

The Jardon House was located on the corner of East Harford Street and Second Street opposite the Laurel Villa in Milford. For many years the Jardon House was a well-respected boardinghouse. In later years it was known as the "Hillcrest." (Collection of the Pike County Historical Society.)

The Mayflower Hotel was a popular dining establishment in the Borough of Milford. Many will remember it by its later name "The Coachman's Inn." It was located south of Dimmick Inn on what is now a vacant lot. (Courtesy of Howard Brunhoelzl.)

Samuel Dimmick built the Dimmick House in 1829. It burned in the 1850s and was rebuilt with brick by the Dimmick family. It has served the public for over 150 years and has been designated a historic site on the Commonwealth's Historic Site Registry. Perhaps its most famed proprietor was Fannie Dimmick who was described as a "character." She wore masculine attire, enjoyed fly fishing and riding, and was described in an article in the local paper as being "like the waterfalls, mountains and trout streams (she) is one of the attractions of Pike County and she is the biggest hearted woman ever born in the Delaware Valley." The Dimmick is located on Harford Street in Milford and is presently owned and operated by Gerry Hansen and Ed and Karen Leschorn. (Collection of the Pike County Historical Society.)

This is a postcard of the Dimmick Inn on the corner of Harford and Broad Streets in Milford as it appeared in the 1940s when owned by the Friend family. (Collection of the Pike County Historical Society.)

Depicted is a stereoscope picture taken in the 1890s of the original Vantine Hotel, which was located at the end of Ninth Street in Milford Township. It is the present home of Ron Parkers. (Collection of the Pike County Historical Society.)

The other Vantine Hotel, located in Milford at the intersection of Harford Street and Sawkill Avenue where the Eckerd drugstore is now, was built by John Beck in the late 1800s. It was known as the "farmer's hotel" and it was a stopping place for farmers from the outlying townships coming into Milford on business. The property boasted a large barn, an icehouse, a large manicured lawn, a grape arbor, and many fruit trees. The property changed hands many times over the years until it was finally purchased by Albert Luhrs in 1973. The hotel was leveled and a new building was erected to house Luhrs Hardware Store. (Courtesy of Christine Richards.)

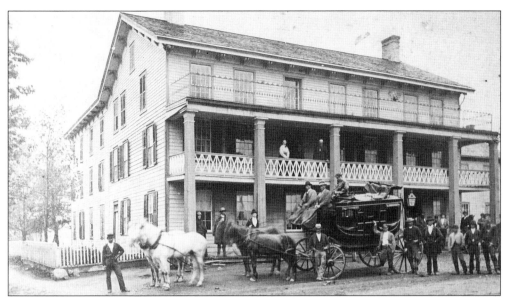

The Crissman House was located where Rite Aid drugstore is now at the corner of West Harford and Broad Streets in Milford. It was built in 1826 by Timothy Candee and was called the Pike County House. In 1853, Cyrus Crissman bought it and renamed it the Crissman House. In 1876, his son Frank took over the management and added rooms. Frank was a very political figure in the county and the hotel became the headquarters for the Pike County Democratic Party. The hotel burned in 1960. (Collection of the Pike County Historical Society.)

The Sawkill House was reputed to be one of Milford's first hotels. At one time, Millicent Crissman held dancing classes every Saturday afternoon there, and the ballroom of the hotel was used as a school until the new school at the northeast corner of Fourth and Ann was ready. In 1912, film director D.W. Griffith came to Milford to film two "moving pictures:" *The Informer*, a Civil War story, and *A Feud in the Kentucky Hills*. Many members of his acting troupe including Dorothy and Lillian Gish, Mary Pickford, Blanche Sweet, and Walter Miller stayed at the Sawkill House. The building at 202 East Harford Street is all that remains of the Sawkill House. (Collection of the Pike County Historical Society.)

Louis Fauchere immigrated to New York City around 1850 and worked as a chef at Delmonico's Restaurant. Some time later, Fauchere was able to leave the city and build a hotel/restaurant in Milford. Chef Fauchere's cuisine was well received by local people as well as wealthy summer visitors. When Louis had amassed enough money, he closed his business in the winter months and took yearly trips to Europe and returned to Milford each spring with new recipes. In one instance he returned with a billiard table, the first ever in Pike County. After his death, his widow asked only one thing of their children who continued to operate the business: that they should never again serve Chicken Marengo in the restaurant, because no one could make it like he did. Her wish was honored. In the mid-1980s, Lewis Miller bought the property and renovated the building, and it sits proudly on Broad Street in Milford today. This photograph was taken *c*. 1870. (Collection of the Pike County Historical Society.)

This 1900 photograph, taken at the back of the Hotel Fauchere, shows its beautiful lawns where there is now a parking lot. (Collection of the Pike County Historical Society.)

The Tom Quick Inn on Broad Street in Milford was originally two hotels; the Centre Square Hotel pictured here, and to the right, hidden by the trees, the Terwilliger House. From 1945 to 1950, Bob Phillips Sr. joined the properties and created the Tom Quick. The Centre Square Hotel was built in 1882 by George Dauman. It boasted modern conveniences of steam heat, hot and cold water, and a bar. Dauman also built and ran the Terwilliger House, and both establishments were renowned for their excellent food enhanced by herbs and condiments raised in a large garden behind the hotels. The hotels were a frequent destination for bicyclists from Port Jervis and surrounding areas. The Tom Quick Inn is owned by Richard and Pam Lutfy and is open to the public. (Courtesy of Richard Lutfy.)

This is a 1930s postcard of the Collinwood Inn on Broad Street in Milford. It was operated for many years by Maurice and Peg May as a boardinghouse. This property is now a parking lot across from the house known as "The Columns." (Courtesy of Jim May.)

Here is a rare photograph c. 1875 of Judge George Heller and his family outside the Harford House, the oldest building in Milford Borough, on East Harford Street. The Harford House was built more than two hundred years ago by Robert Harford of Philadelphia before the village of Milford was laid out by founder John Biddis, who also owned the home in the last years of the 18th century. The most notable owner of the Harford House was Dr. Francis Smith who came to America during the Revolutionary War. It is reputed that General Lafayette, his close friend, visited him here while on his way to New York City. Today this post-Colonial building is operated as a Bed and Breakfast Inn. (Collection of the Pike County Historical Society.)

The Homestead, pictured here in 1899 at the end of Fourth Street in Milford, was burned to the ground by arsonist fire in 1975. The hotel was an imposing four-story structure with shaded covered porches on two levels and had a capacity for one hundred guests. It was built in the late 1800s by Abram D. Brown, a local entrepreneur and a one-time director of the Milford National Bank. The Homestead provided visitors with a spacious dance floor and swimming facilities on the Vandermark Creek. (Collection of the Pike County Historical Society.)

The Hermitage was located in Milford Township on the top of Fire Tower Road and provided a pleasant retreat from the bustle of Milford. (Courtesy of the Hinkel family.)

One out of the handful of buildings still in existence today is the Brookside Villa. It overlooks the Vandermark Creek near the old stone bridge at the end of Broad Street. It evolved from the farmhouse of John and Louisa Ross Brodhead and was built on the site of the homestead of Frederich Vandermark who settled there in the mid-1700s. A 1910 brochure picture shows the neatly kept villa in an idyllic setting with a latticed dining room extension, a footbridge across the brook, and a summerhouse banked by lilacs. (Courtesy of Mr. and Mrs. William Fleming.)

Two

RIVERS AND SCENES

This is a photograph of the Delaware River in Milford below the Bluff House Hotel. For over 250 years the Delaware has served as a source of transportation and a form of recreation. The river continues to be an important part of the community. This 1940s view shows the river at the Milford bend looking towards Montague, New Jersey. (Collection of the Pike County Historical Society.)

This is an early 20th-century photograph of Sawyer's Pond (Sawkill Creek), created by the Wells Dam at the foot of Broad Street in Milford. This was a favorite place for ice-skating and boating before the dam was washed away by the Flood of 1955. (Courtesy of Mr. and Mrs. William McGaughey.)

Depicted is a view of Wright's Bridge during the 1920s looking toward Milford. In the distance can be seen the present-day Lender Home on the corner of Broad Street and Water Street. (Courtesy of Kitty Myer.)

This is the bridge at Metz's Ice Plant on Lower Broad Street during the Flood of 1903. The two-story home on the right is the present-day home of Virginia Kidd. The second man from the left is Harold Burnett and the third man is William Metz. (Collection of the Pike County Historical Society.)

Seen here is a picture taken c. 1900 of the Wells Fanning Mill factory where excelsior was manufactured on the Sawkill Creek. This creek was a favorite spot for fishing, hiking, and picnicking. This area is known locally as "Milford Glen." (Collection of the Pike County Historical Society.)

35

This incredible photograph of visitors enjoying the cascading Sawkill Falls at Grey Towers in Milford Township was taken in 1889. One hundred and nine years later these magnificent falls still attract thousands of visitors. (Collection of the Pike County Historical Society.)

The following was written in a 1901 advertisement for Pike County: "The scenery in the county is equal to any on this continent or Europe." This young boy enjoying a summer day on the millpond with the beautiful mountains in the background elegantly illustrates this thought. Scenes like these continue to attract visitors from all over the world to this area. (Courtesy of William Kiger.)

This turn-of-the-century photograph was taken of the Vandermark Creek Bridge. Built in 1867, the bridge served as the entranceway to the Borough of Milford for many years. (Collection of the Pike County Historical Society.)

Depicted is a silent movie scene from *A Feud in the Kentucky Hills* with Harry Carey, Lillian Gish, Henry Walhal, and Blanche Sweet on the Delaware River in 1912. This area was frequently used for the production of films due to the region's mountain ridges where cactus and other desert-type vegetation grew. The grand views of the New Jersey Kittatiny Mountains resemble a western landscape. (Collection of the Pike County Historical Society.)

This is a 1930s photograph of the Glenwood Lake Dam and waterwheel in Millrift. From 1924 to 1952 this was the only power source for the residents of Millrift. The cost was $2 a month as long as you provided your own poles and wire. (Collection of the Millrift Civic Association.)

WATER WHEEL
WATER POWER
GLENWOOD LAKE DAM.

This is a 1920 view from Millrift of Cherry Island in the Delaware River. (Collection of the Pike County Historical Society.)

This photograph was taken in 1908 of members of the Gassmann family relaxing on the banks of the Cummings Hill Brook in Westfall Township. (Courtesy of the Gassmann family.)

This is a 1914 scene of the beautiful Shohola Falls. (Collection of the Minisink Valley Historical Society.)

Three
TRANSPORTATION

The Hiawatha Stagecoach was used from 1840 to 1890 and was operated by the Findlay family. They transported passengers and delivered mail from Milford to Port Jervis, even over the frozen Delaware River. Findlay came from Scotland where he once drove for Queen Victoria during her visits to Scotland. Restored in 1982, the coach is on display at the Pike County Historical Society at 608 Broad Street, Milford. (Collection of the Minisink Valley Historical Society.)

Before the bridges were built secure enough to withstand flooding, people up and down the Delaware River relied on the ferry. This ferry service was put back into use after the 1903 "Pumpkin Flood" that destroyed bridges between Matamoras, Pennsylvania, and Port Jervis, New York. (Courtesy of Bill Schneider.)

This is a picture of the second Barrett Bridge across the Delaware River looking from Port Jervis towards Matamoras. Prior to 1906, this was a toll bridge. The cost was 2¢ for a pedestrian and 40¢ for each wagon. By 1922, due to political controversies, all tolls were ceased. (Courtesy of Richard and Shirley Basham.)

Out with the old and in with the new! This shows the opening of the fourth Barrett Bridge between Matamoras and Port Jervis and the dismantling of the third Barrett Bridge in 1939. (Courtesy of Richard and Shirley Basham.)

Depicted here is the building of the Shohola-Greeley Road in 1932. (Courtesy of Mr. and Mrs. Edward Hess.)

The Erie Railroad Station in Shohola was originally built in the early 1860s and redesigned over the years. The station was abandoned in 1964 and razed in 1974. (Courtesy of the Hinkel family.)

This postcard of Parkers Glen bluestone dock is from the early 1900s. Anything left of Parkers Glen was washed away in the Flood of 1955. (Courtesy of the Hinkel family.)

This is Shohola Glen's main railroad station in the 1890s. At its peak, one hundred thousand people visited the glen annually. For $1, tourists made the 100-mile journey in four hours from New York City. When they arrived here, the tourists would enjoy some of the most beautiful scenery in the Northeast, an amusement park, dining, dancing and skating facilities, and a switchback railroad. (Courtesy of Andrew Monisera.)

Seen here is the Shohola Glen railroad station in the glen c. 1895. The glen operated between 1881 and 1907. (Courtesy of Andrew Monisera.)

This is an 1890s photograph of a train car used on the Shohola Glen switchback railroad. (Courtesy of Andrew Monisera.)

This view of the switchback railroad in Shohola Glen was taken *c.* 1890. The switchback was used to transport tourists from the main railroad station to the glen entrance 1 mile downhill for 5¢. (Collection of the Minisink Valley Historical Society.)

This sawmill, built in the 1790s, was used to lift the railroad cars up from the glen and back to the main station. (Courtesy of Andrew Monisera.)

Here folks are waiting for the train at the Erie Station in Pond Eddy *c.* 1890. This southern Shohola village was once called "Flagstone," the center of the area's prosperous bluestone industry. (Collection of the Minisink Valley Historical Society.)

This is a bluestone mine in 1914 near Millrift Railroad crossing. John Fletcher Kilgour commenced bluestone quarrying in 1863. By 1870, Kilgour had formed the New York-Pennsylvania Bluestone Company, and its major stockholders were Jay Gould, James Fisk, and New York City Mayor Boss Tweed, of Tammany Hall fame. Many New York, Philadelphia, and Havana, Cuba sidewalks were made using Pike County bluestone. (Collection of the Millrift Civic Association.)

Rafting down the river was a strenuous occupation. This method of transporting lumber downstream to Philadelphia and Trenton began as early as 1764 with the last raft carrying goods in 1924. (Courtesy of Bill Schneider.)

This is a view from the Hawks Nest of a train chugging through Millrift along the Delaware River. (Courtesy of Bill Schneider.)

This is a 1950s postcard showing the old and new Milford/Montague bridges. (Courtesy of Joe Herbert.)

This is the Matamoras Railroad Bridge at Loder Street (Avenue C). This bridge was built in 1898 with hopes of bringing rail travel from Port Jervis, New York to Stroudsburg, Pennsylvania. This dream was lost in 1903 when the bridge was demolished by floodwaters stranding two locomotives in Matamoras. (Courtesy of Richard and Shirley Basham.)

This 1914 photograph is of Westfall Township in the vicinity of the firehouse on Route 209, looking towards Avenue C. During this period, this area of Westfall consisted of many farms. In the distance can be seen one of the locomotives that was stranded on this side of the river after the bridge collapsed .These locomotives were sold as scrap years later. The building on the right was the Mansion House Hotel. This large hotel accommodated 150 guests and was located on Tenth Street in Matamoras. It was destroyed by fire in 1928. (Edward B. Watson Collection, courtesy of Allan Berner.)

Was this the first Milford taxi? This photograph was taken in the early 1900s in front of the Hotel Fauchere with Jake Shorr, a Civil War veteran, at the reins. (Courtesy of Mr. and Mrs. Harry Buchannan.)

This 1912 scene on lower Broad Street in Milford illustrates how sledding was a form of winter transportation in the area. (Collection of the Pike County Historical Society.)

Cruising through the Pike County countryside was very pleasant in 1909. Here the Kyte's of Milford motor along without a bit of traffic in sight. (Collection of the Pike County Historical Society.)

This bridge located at Bob's Beach in Milford was removed in the mid-1950s when the new toll bridge was completed. The old bridge abutments can still be seen on the New Jersey side of the Delaware River. (Collection of the Minisink Valley Historical Society.)

In the late 18th century, the only way to travel from Milford to Stroudsburg was by a horse-drawn coach. Here the three-teamed Palace Car gets ready for another run. (Collection of the Pike County Historical Society.)

This photograph was taken on the corner of East Harford Street and Blackberry Alley showing the first passenger touring cars in Milford. The gentleman on the right is John A. Watts. (Collection of the Pike County Historical Society.)

Four

FARMING

This is the Gassmann family farm in Westfall *c.* 1906. In that era, there were approximately 869 commercial farms in Pike County. By 1958, only 204 farms were in operation. Farms supplied produce to the many hotels and boardinghouses in and around Pike County. (Courtesy of Richard Gassmann.)

William Quinn arrived in Dingman Township in 1817 from Ireland. Here he purchased 300 acres of land and began the Quinn family tradition of dairy farming. More than 180 years later, this remains one of the last surviving farms in Pike County. (Courtesy of the Quinn family.)

This is a photograph of longtime Dingman Township farmer Julius Kiesel. Mr. Kiesel was born in 1872 and lived to be 101 years old. His farm was located on Kiesel Road in Dingman Township and was in operation for many years. (Collection of the Pike County Historical Society.)

This is an aerial view showing Indian Point House Resort and the Hotel Schanno surrounded by miles of farmlands. In the distance is Minisink Island, which has been farmed for centuries. (Courtesy of Barbara Orben.)

This view is from the cliffs in Westfall Township c. 1906 of farmlands. This is looking towards the present-day site of the Delaware Valley School Complex and shopping areas. In the distance, the Rockview in Montague, New Jersey, can be seen. (Courtesy of Richard Gassmann.)

This is Ed Hess of Shohola mowing his fields on his John Deere tractor in the 1940s. (Courtesy of Mr. and Mrs. Edward Hess.)

This is an early postcard of Sunset Farm in Walker Lake in Shohola. In later years, this was operated as a bar and restaurant known as Hickey's Sunset Farm on Little Walker Lake Road. (Courtesy of the Hinkel family.)

Posing are Ruben and Edward Bell, owners of the Bell Farm in front of their greenhouses in 1903. Today these greenhouses are operated by Jeff and Donna Mance of Jeff's Garden Shop on Avenue M between Fourth and Fifth Streets in Matamoras Borough. (Courtesy of Margaret Fuller.)

The Bell Farm in Matamoras was comprised of 150 acres and was located on the present-day Airport Park Recreation Area. In the distance, St. Mary's Church on Ball Street in Port Jervis, New York, can be seen. (Courtesy of Margaret Fuller.)

This picture shows the Ruben P. Bell Homestead built in the 1880s. This house is located on the site of the Tri-State Canoes in Westfall Township. (Courtesy of Margaret Fuller.)

This is a 1940s photograph of Model Farm located on Route 209/River Road in Dingman Township. In 1850, Ebenezer Warner began farming on this land. The silo can still be seen on the National Park Service Land. (Courtesy of Richard Snyder.)

This photograph was taken in 1916 on Grandma Gebhardt's 70th birthday. The Gebhardt Farm was started in 1869. It was comprised of 100 acres situated near the present-day Mount Haven Restaurant in Dingman Township. As shown in this photograph, many generations are gathered together for this event. The following are listed from left to right: (front row) Isabel DuBois Kramer, Juliette Boileau, Sadie Boileau Bensley, Ina Drake Harmon, Hilda Drake Stoyan, and Arthur DuBois; (second row) Willie DuBois, Nellie Gebhardt DuBois, Katie Gebhardt Boileau, Godfrey Gebhardt, Pauline Ott Gebhardt, Annie Gebhardt Drake, and Carla Gebhardt DuBois; (third row) Pauline Boileau (Merritt Quinn's mother), Charlie Boileau (Merritt Quinn's grandfather), Minnie Boileau, Lizzie Gebhardt, Charles Gebhardt, Christopher Gebhardt, and Henry Gebhardt; (back row) Charlie Foster, Minnie G. Foster, twin boys—Fred and Ed Gebhardt. This family farm was sold in 1950.

Depicted is a 1900s view of the Orchards in Milford Township, the original Stumpf Homestead. The man standing in the driveway is Julio Stumpf, grandfather of Julio Santos, who is the young boy sitting to the right. This property is now owned by Richard Snyder who operates his llama farm on Foster Hill Road. (Courtesy of Richard Snyder.)

This is an early 1900s view of the Foster Hill Dairy Farm operated by the Stumpf and Santos families for generations. The high elevation of this property made this land ideal for growing apples as the cold winds descended into the valley, thus the name "The Orchards." (Courtesy of Richard Snyder.)

Five
MAIN STREET

This building in a 1905 picture was initially a one-half story building on the corner of Broad and West Catherine Street, Milford, dating from the 1700s. At that time it was known as the Plank House Inn when Plank Road ran from Milford to Scranton. It was enlarged in the mid-1800s and renamed the "Alpine" and operated as an inn by Nellie Rupp until it closed due to Prohibition. Later it was the first A&P in town. In the early 1990s it was destroyed by fire and replaced by the existing building. (Collection of the Pike County Historical Society.)

Built about 1905 by Joseph A Schroeder, this general merchandise store operated as the first post office in Matamoras. For many years it was known as "Jay's Handy Corner" and was owned by Jay Schroeder, Pike County commissioner from 1944 to 1969. By 1975 it became the "Mayors Corner," when Mayor Joe Ricciardi of Matamoras purchased the property. (Courtesy of Bill Schneider.)

This is the Vandermark Hotel *c.* 1950, a once popular Broad Street bar and grill in Milford. Built in the 1700s, the first court of Pike and Wayne Counties was held here when the building was owned by George Bowhannon (Buchanan) in 1785. The building was razed in the 1980s to make way for the Pike County Administration Building. (Courtesy of Barbara Orben.)

Welcome to J.E. Tobin's dry goods and grocery store in the late 1800s. This building, in the heart of Milford's commercial district, was home for many years to Leonard's Five and Dime. (Collection of the Pike County Historical Society.)

Pictured here is J.F. Malony's General Merchandise Store on Bluestone Boulevard in Millrift. Maloney was a busy man, acting as postmaster, ticket agent, baggage handler, and manager for the Erie Railroad. He served as town clerk, worked in real estate, founded the Literary Society, and wrote articles for Milford and Port Jervis newspapers. (Collection of the Millrift Civic Association.)

This photograph shows Millrift Hotel guests waiting in front of the Millrift General Store and Post Office, for the train to New York, c. 1905. (Collection of the Millrift Civic Association.)

This is a picture of main street Shohola *c*. 1920 on a beautiful autumn day on Richardson Avenue. (Courtesy of Andrew Monisera.)

This is a 1930s view of Broad Street gazing up at Greenwood Hills in Milford Township, prior to the construction of Route 209 and the present-day entrance to the borough. (Collection of the Pike County Historical Society.)

The Riverside Dairy was located on Delaware Drive in Matamoras. This photograph shows Milton Shay delivering milk in 1900 along the Delaware River. (Courtesy of Mr. and Mrs. Richard Basham.)

This depicts William Angle's Blacksmith shop on East Catherine and Fifth Streets in Milford. This photograph was taken during the first years of the 20th century. Please notice the steeple of the Episcopal church in the background. (Collection of the Pike County Historical Society.)

This photograph shows the popular barbershop on the corner of Broad and East Catherine Streets in Milford. Please note the hand-painted barber pole c. 1905. This is the present-day location of the Milford Auto Body Shop. (Collection of the Pike County Historical Society.)

This photograph taken in 1894 shows the Silver Springs Brewery in Dingman Township. It was the first manufacturer of bottled beer for home consumption in America. The stone brewery produced beer from 1840 to 1875. In 1890, the brewery was demolished and the 40-room resort called Silver Spring House was built. (Courtesy of Mr. and Mrs. Richard Lutfy.)

This is a 1930s ad campaign for Atlantic Richfield White Flash Gas at C.W. Dunkers Service Station at the corner of Pennsylvania Avenue and Third Street in Matamoras. This business is presently owned by William Schneider. (Courtesy of William Schneider.)

This photograph depicts a typical store of early Matamoras. It is thought to be the Martin Heller Tobacco Store. Here cigars were manufactured from tobacco that had been dried on the back porch of the store. (Courtesy of William Schneider.)

This is a 1940s picture of Forest Hall. The hall's original bluestone section was built in the 1880s by Calvert Vaux. It served as Milford's post office and as a drugstore. In 1904 James Pinchot had the latter part of Forest Hall designed and built by Hunt and Hunt as a gift to his son, Gifford Pinchot. Forest Hall's second floor became the first Yale School of Forestry, while the first floor was utilized by local businesses, as it still is today. (Courtesy of Barbara Orben.)

This 1940s postcard shows the Sun Dial Tourist Station on Route 6 and 209 in Milford Township. The building in the center is the present-day restaurant "The Inn at the Edge of the Forest." (Courtesy of Barbara Orben.)

Welcome to Tuttle's General Store at the intersection of Twin Lakes Road and Woodtown Road in Shohola Township. This is now the location of the Le Gorille Restaurant. For many years it was operated as a local tavern by Harley Hinkel. (Courtesy of the Hinkel family.)

In this photograph we see Bob Blood helping a customer at the Atlantic Gas Station located on the way to his Delaware River Beach in Dingman Township in 1930. (Courtesy of Bob Blood.)

Some local folks are cruising around town in the 1930s on Broad Street in Milford. Pictured here from left to right are Fred Herbst Jr., Thornton Ryder, and Theodore Herbst. (Courtesy of Fred Herbst.)

This is an 1890s postcard looking up East Harford Street in Milford. The Dimmick Inn stands on the left, and farther up the Crissman House can be seen. (Collection of the Pike County Historical Society.)

In 1882, Jervis Gordon built this mill along the Sawkill Creek in Milford. The Rowe Brothers purchased the mill in 1904 and continued to operate the mill along with a woodworking shop where they also manufactured wooden souvenirs. Today the mill is divided into small quaint shops and the property is owned by Robert Hartman and Leonard Freeman. (Courtesy of Robert Hartman.)

Chance Rowe worked in his blacksmith shop for many years in the historic "Upper Mill." In the 1900s, Rowe also built a massive steel waterwheel and large pulley made of maple cog gears that powered both the mill and the machine shop. Visitors can still see the powerful wheel that continued grinding grain up until the late 1950s. (Collection of the Pike County Historical Society.)

This is a snow-covered street in Milford in the 1930s. This photograph was taken from Herbst's Drugstore, the present day Hartman's Market on Broad Street. The Hotel Fauchere and the Tom Quick Inn are in the background. (Courtesy of Fred Herbst.)

This is the Village Diner in Westfall Township as shown in 1958. It still welcomes tourists passing through as well as serving the local townspeople. Very few of these stainless steel structures remain today. (Courtesy of Ethel Musselwhite.)

The Milford Diner opened for business in 1929. This photograph taken in 1946 shows the original structure on the corner of East Ann and Broad Streets in Milford Borough. (Courtesy of Ethel Musselwhite.)

This is a 1910 postcard of Forest Hall on Broad Street in Milford. (Courtesy of the Hinkel family.)

Seen here is a 1930s postcard of West High Street in Milford. On the front lawn of the Pike County Courthouse stood the Civil War mortars. These cannons were placed there in 1896. In 1942, they were sold as scrap metal for the war effort. (Courtesy of Mr. and Mrs. William McGaughey.)

This building once stood on Broad Street in Milford across from Hartman's Market. It housed a photograph shop and later an electrical shop. The sign on the right advertises a movie showing at the Strand Theater in Port Jervis, New York, around 1930. (Courtesy of Fred Herbst.)

These buildings were located on Pennsylvania Avenue next to the present-day Mellon Bank in Matamoras. This photograph shows Jack's Sweet Shoppe where one could purchase homemade ice cream and candy. (Courtesy of William Schneider.)

The Marford Silk Mill, first incorporated in 1920 by Martin and Sanford, provided Matamoras with a thriving industry for more than 40 years. This building still stands on the corner of Fifth Street and Avenue G. (Courtesy of Skip and Lorraine Gregory.)

This photograph shows Pennsylvania Avenue in Matamoras during the summer of 1947. Jay's Handy Corner is shown on the right. (Courtesy of Jayne Schroeder Manzer.)

This photograph depicts the 1927 filming of the movie *The Strength of the Weak*. Local residents worked as extras during a bank robbery scene. The building that served as the bank is the present-day Masonic Hall Building on Fourth Street in Milford. Milford residents include George Funk, Donald Martin, Jack Findlay, Frank Ludwig, Lee Thursby, Frank Le Compte, Roswell Palmer, Francis Custis, Clarence DeWitt, and Barney Canne. (Collection of the Pike County Historical Society.)

This photograph shows Seymour's Coal Yard between First and Second Streets in Matamoras. Horse-drawn carriages delivered coal to local residents for many years from this yard. (Courtesy of William Schneider.)

This picture shows Mitchell's General Store on the corner of West Ann and Broad Streets in Milford. The house on the left was Arthur Mitchell's home and it was moved in the late 1920s to East Harford Street and placed next to the Dimmick Inn. (Collection of the Pike County Historical Society.)

This 1940s photograph of Broad and West Ann Street in Milford shows Emma Wolfe's Tea Room which eventually became Elmer's Coffee Shop. The building was razed to allow for further expansion of the First National Bank of Pike County, now the present-day Corestates Bank. (Courtesy of Barbara Orben.)

This is a photograph of Louis Monisera in 1932 making a delivery to Rohman's Hotel in Shohola. (Courtesy of Andrew Monisera.)

Depicted here is the Ryman and Wells Store on East Harford Street in Milford. It was operated until the early part of the 20th century. This is the present-day location of Progressive Health. (Collection of the Pike County Historical Society.)

This photograph shows the exterior of Kyte's store on the corner of East Ann and Broad Streets in Milford where a parking lot is now located for R&S Jewelry. Howard Kyte poses in 1898. (Collection of the Pike County Historical Society.)

Seen here is proprietor Ben Kyte (Howard's son) working in the store during the early 1920s. (Collection of the Pike County Historical Society.)

In the 1930s, a Wells Fargo office served Milford Borough. This is the present-day site of the Milford Firehouse on West Catherine Street. (Collection of the Pike County Historical Society.)

Welcome to Fritz Suessman's Shohola Meat Market in 1935 in the back of Rohman's Hotel. Listed from left to right are Fritz Suessman, Gus Hoehne, Louis Monisera, and Albert Schoner. (Courtesy of Andrew Monisera.)

Six

CHURCHES AND SCHOOLS

The Methodist Episcopal Church on the corner of Avenue H and Third Street in Matamoras was built in 1889. In 1916, the chapel was remodeled and the building was elevated to make room for the basement to be used for Sunday school and as a fellowship hall for church suppers. The name was changed to Epworth Methodist Church. When the United Brethen and the Methodist conferences merged, the name was changed again to the present-day name of the United Methodist Church of Matamoras. (Courtesy of Richard and Shirley Basham.)

The Episcopal Church of the Good Shepherd on the corner of West Catherine and Fifth Streets in Milford was built in 1872. An Episcopal Sunday school had already been established in 1866. Like other Milford congregations without a church, services had previously been held in the old stone courthouse. This structure was destroyed by fire in 1913 and the present stone church was constructed. (Collection of the Pike County Historical Society.)

This shows the ladies of the Good Shepherd Episcopal Church at a church festival in the 1930s. Mabel Luhrs (Al Luhrs mother) is sitting next to the driver. Behind the driver is Mabel Ryder Schroeder. (Courtesy of Jayne Schroeder Manzer.)

St. Joseph's Church between Third and Fourth Streets on Avenue F in Matamoras was built in 1894. Pastors of this church served at Shohola, Parkers Glen, Pond Eddy, and Lackawaxen during the years of 1899 to 1928. This church was replaced by the present church in 1970. (Courtesy of St. Joseph's Church.)

Seen here is the dedication for the building of the new St. Patrick's Church in 1956 on East High Street in Milford. This church replaced the one on Eighth Street that was built in 1874 and is today a private residence. Pictured in the center are Reverend Vincent Mahon, pastor of St. Patrick's Church, and the two altar boys, Edward Lilley and Mark Yarros. (Courtesy of St. Patrick's Church.)

St. Ann's Catholic Church erected in 1924, is located in the heart of the Shohola village. Before this church was built, Catholic services were held in St. Jacobi's Lutheran Church. (Courtesy of Andrew Monisera.)

St. Jacobi's Lutheran Church was built in 1871 in Shohola on land donated by Chauncey Thomas, owner of the Shohola Hotel, and John F. Kilgour, the "Bluestone King." At the entrance of St. Jacobi's lies one of the largest bluestone slabs ever taken from the quarry. (Courtesy of Andrew Monisera.)

This postcard from 1925 depicts both Presbyterian churches of Milford. The original church was constructed in the early 1800s and replaced in 1874 by the existing church. This photograph was taken in 1875. (Collection of the Pike County Historical Society.)

1825   100th Anniversary   1925

First Presbyterian Church
Milford, Pike Co., Pa.

The Old Church and the New Church

This shows the present First Presbyterian Church erected in 1875 on the corner of Broad and West Ann Streets in Milford. In 1886, Lt. Gov. William Bross of Illinois, in memory of his parents who were some of the church's first founders, donated the bell and the clock to the congregation. This has been a longtime landmark in the Borough of Milford. (Collection of the Pike County Historical Society.)

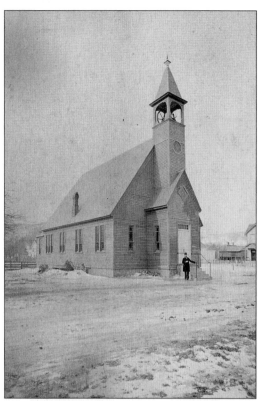

The Hope Evangelical Church on Avenue G in Matamoras was built in 1892. This photograph was taken shortly after its completion. (Courtesy of the Hope Church.)

The present-day St. Patrick's Rectory on the corner of East High and Fourth Streets in Milford was home for many years to the Sisters of the Immaculate Heart of Mary. Between the years 1946 and 1978, the sisters taught kindergarten to many area children. Here we have a 1950s photograph of the children dressed up for Halloween. (Courtesy of Bill Kiger.)

This schoolhouse in Shohola was built in 1916. During the 1920s, grades 1-12 were taught in this two-room schoolhouse. Today the building serves as the Shohola Municipal Hall. (Courtesy of Andrew Monisera.)

This is the eighth grade graduating class of 1956. This class became part of the first four-year class of the Delaware Valley High School. Pictured third in from left is Beth Nikles. Next to her is MaryAnn Malhame and far right is Andrew Monisera. (Courtesy of Andrew Monisera.)

Pictured here is the Woodtown School on Parkers Glen Road in Shohola in the 1920s. During that time in Pike County, each municipality had its own schoolhouse. (Courtesy of Mr. and Mrs. Edward Hess.)

This is the Quicktown School in 1910. Pictured standing from left to right are as follows: (front row) unidentified, Bob Blood, and Bruce Cuddeback; (back row) Edna Blood, unidentified, Teacher Charlotte Stark, George Miller, Ralph Gassmann, and Russell Decker. This building is located next to the Westfall Professional Building on Route 6 and 209 and is the present day residence of Carmella Cicerone. (Courtesy of Richard Gassmann.)

From the years of 1879 through 1924, this building served as the Matamoras High School. It is located at 210 Avenue G and it is the present-day Tri-State Christian Fellowship. (Courtesy of the Matamoras Alumni Association.)

Matamoras High School was constructed in 1923 on the corner of Sixth and Avenue H. It served in this capacity until 1956 when it became the Matamoras Elementary School. Razed in the mid-1990s, it is the location of Pike County's first senior citizen housing complex, Delaware Run. (Courtesy of the Matamoras Alumni Association.)

In 1976, the one-room red Schocopee Schoolhouse was moved from its original location on Firetower Road to Apple Valley Village on Route 6 in Milford Township. Although the date of its construction remains unknown, it was most likely built in the late 1800s. The last classes were held in 1907. (Courtesy of Sandy Leiser.)

The Milford High School was built in 1904 on the corner of West Harford and Fifth Streets. It replaced the former school that stood on West Catherine Street across from the Borough Hall. In later years, the bluestone building served as the elementary school. Today the former school bell can be seen in the Department of Education Building in Washington, D.C. (Courtesy of Fred Herbst.)

Seven

Civic Groups and Leisure Time

This is a picture of the original Pike County Courthouse as it appeared in 1885. In 1814, after Pike County had been recently formed, the residents of Milford raised $1,500 for the completion of this unique building by Daniel Dimmick with cobbled fieldstones. Before Milford had churches, this beautiful courthouse was used for religious services. In 1871, due to an increase in population, the old courthouse became the county jail until the 1990s when the new prison was built in Blooming Grove. Today this historic structure, the second oldest courthouse in Pennsylvania, houses the Pike County Sheriff's Department. (Collection of the Pike County Historical Society.)

During WW II, a civil defense post was located at Matamoras Airport. This airplane spotter post was manned from 1941 to 1945. Pictured from left to right are Dick Jeffries, Edith Strait, Nial Warner, and William Weintz. (Courtesy of the Matamoras Fire Department.)

Matamoras Airport was established in 1929, and by 1938, with WPA assistance, the airport had two paved and lighted runways each over one-quarter of a mile long. During WW II, Zeke Dervend, a Matamoras resident, trained Air Force "cadets" and operated a flying school at Matamoras Airport. This photograph was taken c. 1945. (Courtesy of Jim Crawford.)

In the 1940s, Litts's Air Service provided repair and maintenance on aircraft at the Matamoras Airport. Pictured here fifth and sixth from the left are Jim Crawford and Bob Litts. (Courtesy of Jim Crawford.)

This is a 1909 postcard of the Homestead Free Library located at 201 Broad Street, Milford. The building was erected in 1824 as the original home of the Pinchot family. In 1900, the building started being used as a library. In 1923, the Pinchot's deeded the property to the Community House Association. (Courtesy of the Hinkel family.)

In this 1930s photograph in Matamoras, the Christmas Basket Committee is getting ready to deliver flour and other food staples to the local residents for the holidays. The members belonged to the American Legion. (Courtesy of William Clark.)

In the 1940s, women were very involved in local organizations. Here in 1949 is the Ladies Auxiliary of the Matamoras Hose Company. (Courtesy of the Matamoras Fire Department.)

This is a picture of the Milford Fire Company in 1927. These are some members posing in front of the original firehouse on Catharine Street. This building now serves as the Milford Borough Hall. (Collection of the Pike County Historical Society.)

This is a photograph of the Milford Fire Department marching on Broad Street in Milford during the 1899 Fourth of July parade. (Collection of the Pike County Historical Society.)

In the early 1900s the Hess boys of Shohola play a rousing game of baseball. (Collection of Mr. and Mrs. Edward Hess.)

This photograph shows "Smoky Joe" Wood warming up before a game at Fenway Park in Boston, Massachusetts. Joe Wood was raised in Shohola in the Woodtown area. As a pitcher, Smoky Joe led the Red Sox to a World Series victory in 1912. (Collection of the Pike County Historical Society.)

Baseball was a favorite pastime in the early part of the century, as can be seen in this 1910 scene taken at the Milford Ballpark. Note the large grandstands in the background. (Collection of the Pike County Historical Society.)

This is a photograph of the Milford Women's Bowling League at the Port Jervis Bowl in 1953. Listed from left to right are as follows: (first row) Bernetta Misenhelder, Marge Fisher, Kate Stone Williams, and Aggie Stone Geiger; (second row) Mildred Wycoff Craft, Alberta Vandermark Churchill, Centa Quinn Jr., Ada Greening, and Gert Geiger; (third row) Centa Quinn, Hilda Luhrs, Gwen Crellin, Mary Lilley Blitz, Alice Murphy, Lillian Nearing, and Elise Lehde; (fourth row) Ma Stewart, Dot Brunhoelzl, Stella Johns, Myra Clark, Verna Miller, Joanna Antener, and Flo Hinkel. (Courtesy of Howard Brunhoelzl.)

In 1872, the Pike County commissioners hired architect George Barton of Paterson, New Jersey and local entrepreneur A.D. Brown to construct a new courthouse. The original fieldstone structure built in 1814 could no longer serve the booming population, and at first a temporary building was erected on this site. The new courthouse was completed in 1874 at a cost of $45,000 and continues to serve the citizens of Pike County in Milford Borough. The unique architectural style is known as the "French Renaissance" or "General Grant." (Collection of the Pike County Historical Society.)

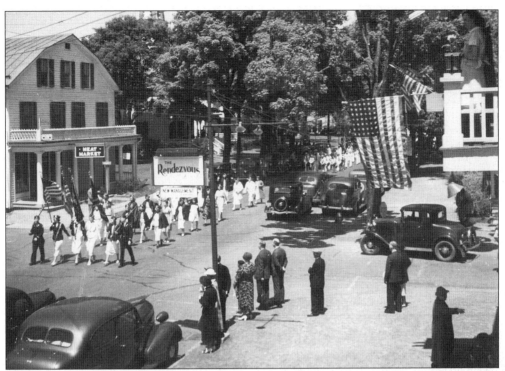

Seen here is a 1940s parade along Broad Street in Milford. (Courtesy of Tom Hoff.)

During the heyday of the hotel and boardinghouse era, parades were a popular summertime activity. This photograph shows a 1920s parade on West Harford Street in Milford. The house in the center of the picture is the present-day Pike County Licensing Bureau. (Courtesy of Bill Kiger.)

This photograph shows an early Fourth of July parade along Broad Street in Milford with the Pike County Courthouse in the foreground. (Collection of the Pike County Historical Society.)

Pictured here is Ernest Wood, the first police chief in Milford Borough, posing on West Catherine Street c. 1920.

This photograph commemorates the dedication of the Civil War Memorial at the Pike County Courthouse in 1938. Pictured from left to right are as follows: Mrs. Ethel Barckley, Mrs. Frank P. Ludwig, Mrs. Lafayette Quick, Mrs. Victoria Fields, Mrs. Hotalen, Scoutmaster Clyde Canouse (holding a Civil War flag), Mrs. Josie Ryder, Mrs. John Durling, Mrs. Kate Sayre (widow of a Civil War veteran), and Mrs. Peter Helms (Gold Star mother). (Collection of the Pike County Historical Society.)

This picture shows the Pike County Fife and Drum Corp. organized in 1937 by Charles Foster Sr. This group involved many local youngsters and marched in many parades, including the dedication of the grand opening of the Matamoras Bridge celebration. The group disbanded in 1941 due to the onset of WW II. (Courtesy of Leith Hoffman.)

On September 24, 1963, Pres. John F. Kennedy arrived at Grey Towers in Milford to dedicate the property as "Pinchot Institute for Conservation Studies." (Courtesy of Leith Hoffman.)

Thousands of local citizens attended the ceremonies and cheered as the popular President spoke and dedicated the institute as a living memorial to Gifford Pinchot, "Father of the Forestry Service." (Courtesy of Leith Hoffman.)

Eight
NEIGHBORHOODS

The "Winsor" was designed and built in 1898 by William Armstrong, a renowned architectural engineer responsible for many important buildings in New York City, including St. Bartholomew's Church and Rectory. He was also responsible for an addition to the Museum of Natural History. Armstrong built this unique Victorian home for his family as a summer residence and landscaped gardens reaching from East High Street to the Delaware River. In 1926, Harold Winsor, a superb chef, transformed the "Armstrong Villa" into an exclusive hotel charging up to $35 per week per guest. In 1941, Margaret Duer Judge purchased the house and property for $5,000 and operated a school for mentally-challenged children. In 1972 the present-day owner, Donald Lee Palmer, bought the "Judge School" and converted it into apartments. (Collection of the Pike County Historical Society.)

The massive gray castle, hence known as "Grey Towers," was commissioned to be built in 1886 by James Pinchot. The architect was Richard Morris Hunt, who also designed other well-known buildings such as John Jacob Astor's New York City residence and Cornelius Vanderbilt II "The Breakers" in Newport, Rhode Island. He also designed the base of the Statue of Liberty. This photograph, taken in the 1890s, depicts the property in Milford before landscaping took place. (Collection of the Pike County Historical Society.)

As "Father of Conservation," Gifford Pinchot, former governor of Pennsylvania, had his estate extensively landscaped over the years with grapevines, rose bushes, and apple and cherry trees. Today the beauty of these grounds attracts many visitors to this National Historic site. (Collection of the Pike County Historical Society.)

This stately home, the DeBerlhe Cottage in the 1890s, stood on the corner of Fourth Street and Peach Alley in Milford. In later years it became the residence of Katherine Sheen. Later this building was purchased by St. Patrick's Church and served as the original rectory. In 1961, this large Victorian house with a mansard roof was torn down and the present-day Parish Center on East High Street was erected. (Collection of the Pike County Historical Society.)

This is a later photograph of the DeBerlhe Cottage in the 1940s showing its wrap-around porch. (Courtesy of St. Patrick's Church.)

This elegant home in Matamoras can still be seen on Avenue E between Third and Fourth Streets. In this early 1900s photograph, it was the Heater family homestead. Today it is the residence of Donald and Kathryn Ricciardi. (Courtesy of Monk Rake.)

Depicted here is an early 1900 photograph of the VanGordon residence on Pennsylvania Avenue in Matamoras between Third and Fourth Streets near the Matamoras Water Authority Building. This house is now owned by the Bittle Family. (Courtesy of James Bianchi.)

This home once stood on the corner of West Harford and Mill Streets in Milford. At this site today is the LA Bank. In the late 1980s this house was moved to the lower end of East Catherine Street. (Collection of the Pike County Historical Society.)

Beautiful tree-lined streets were abundant in this 1910 photograph of East Ann Street in Milford. The Milford Inn is the building on the right. (Collection of the Pike County Historical Society.)

The area of the Van Lierde home, also known as the Storybrook Cottage, where the Dwarfs Kill meets the Raymondskill in Dingman Township, was the site of several early industrial ventures. Among them were a cotton mill, a sawmill, and a tannery. During the 1930s Marcel and Cynthia Van Lierde purchased the old mill wheel from the H.B. Wells mill that was located at lower Broad Street in Milford and installed it at their home to provide electricity for their use. (From the Van Lierde Collection-Marc Sorbe.)

This is a 1924 photograph of the F.P. Sawyer residence and Old Mill Dam on the lower end of Broad Street situated on the Sawkill Creek in Milford. This is the present-day home of William and Joanna McGaughey. (Courtesy of Mr. and Mrs. William McGaughey.)

This is a 1914 postcard of Picnic Rock on the Sawkill Creek in Milford. It was a favorite spot for tourists' enjoyment. (Courtesy of the Hinkel family.)

Seen here is a 1906 picture of philosopher Charles Sanders Peirce, with his wife, Juliette, and their maid at Arisbe, their home in Westfall Township on Route 6 and 209. Peirce was a renowned mathematician who founded the School of Pragmatism. (Courtesy of Richard Gassmann.)

This picture shows local residents enjoying a summer day at the Raymondskill in Dingman Township c. 1900. (Courtesy of Betty Lou Dugan.)

This is the "Old Milford Road" near Cummings Hill Road in Westfall Township in 1906. (Courtesy of Richard Gassmann.)

This 1905 postcard shows a horse and carriage on the "Old Milford Road" in the vicinity of the present-day location of "The Trees." The wagon belonged to Gephardt's Bakery. (Courtesy of Richard Gassmann.)

Depicted is an 1880s photograph of the Milford home of Abram D. Brown. Mr. Brown was a successful businessman who was instrumental in the construction of many well-known structures in the area, such as the Bloomgarden Building on Broad Street in Milford. A.D. Brown erected his home on a site along the Vandermark Creek where he operated his tannery. Brown added onto his house to create the "Homestead Hotel." (Collection of the Pike County Historical Society.)

This is a rear view of the Homestead Hotel in 1899. In this photograph an astute eye can see the fragmented remains in the left center of the A.D. Brown original homestead. (Collection of the Pike County Historical Society.)

The Edward G. Bell Mansion was located in Westfall Township and was built at the turn of the century. This stately home was demolished to make way for Route 84. The Bells were owners of a large farm that encompassed all of Matamoras Airport. This photograph shows the Bell family taking off on a drive in the country. (Courtesy of Margaret Fuller.)

The "Old Westfall Stone House" was built in 1740 by Simeone Westfall on First Street in Matamoras. It was used as a fort in the Revolutionary War, and is still standing and overlooks the Delaware River. (Collection of the Pike County Historical Society.)

This early 1900s street scene in the Borough of Matamoras was taken looking towards the Delaware River on Avenue H. On the left is the Epworth Methodist Church and in the distance is Point Peter in Port Jervis, New York. (Courtesy of William Schneider.)

This beautiful home on the corner of Avenue G and First Street in Matamoras is shown here in the 1920s. (Courtesy of James Bianchi.)

The Jacobus Rosenkrans House in Westfall Township sat on the Delaware River in the area that was known as Rosetown. This is where Tom Quick, son of the first settler in Milford, died in 1796. (Courtesy of Sandy Leiser.)

Seen here is a 1929 photograph of Ferne Shay and Helen Carpenter going for a ride on the back of Shay's Riverside Dairy milk truck with Carlton Shay driving. (Courtesy of Richard and Shirley Basham.)

This wonderful 1920s photograph of the present-day Green/Van Tassell home on the corner of East Ann and Fourth Streets captures perfectly the era's splendid Victorian architecture and the graceful shaded streets of Milford. This simple gabled structure was built in the late 1820s when Samuel G. Thrall sold the property to the trustees of the Milford Academy. In 1885, the Board of School Directors of the Independent School District acquired the academy. When it became too crowded for the growing population, it was sold for $950 to John Grassmuk of New York City for his family's summer home. When Grassmuk purchased the Milford Academy it faced Fourth Street, but he decided to renovate this house, and with a team of horses and timber, he turned the large structure to face East Ann Street. In 1915, Pernina Van Tassell purchased the impressive home and transformed it into a comfortable and friendly boardinghouse. During the time when many movies were produced in the area, William Van Tassell ran a livery business at this site and transported the actors to their filming locations. In this photograph c. 1915, visitors pose for local photographer J.A. Myer.

This is a turn-of-the-century photograph of the 110 West Catherine Street home done in the second empire style. This house has not been altered since its construction and today is the home of Ken and Cathy Recchia. (Collection of the Pike County Historical Society.)

This structure at 110 East Harford Street was built in 1814. It was originally believed to be a tavern. In later years it housed a cobbler shop, a bakery, and a grocery store. When this photograph was taken in 1878 the building was owned by James Wallace, a prominent Milford businessman. Presently, this property is owned by James McLain. (Collection of the Pike County Historical Society.)

Pictured here is an early 1900s winter scene of the logging trade along West Harford Street in Milford. The building to the right is the present location of Sportsmen Rendezuous.

Here we see a Milford family going for a winter stroll on lower Broad Street in 1911. The house in the background is located at 103 Broad Street. The homes in this Milford neighborhood all date to the mid- to late 1800s. (Courtesy of Bill Kiger.)

This stereoscope shows the home on the corner of East Harford and Fourth Streets during the 1860s. It was owned by the Wallaces, and was known for many years as the Armstrong House. It was here that the first Milford Borough Council meeting was held. (Collection of the Pike County Historical Society.)

Pictured is the present home of Scott and Karen Cowern located at 800 Broad Street. This 1863 picture shows homeowner John Hissam and his family. (Collection of the Pike County Historical Society.)

This grand home once stood opposite the Camp Sagamore entrance on Twin Lakes Road in Shohola. This stately house was built in 1885 and belonged to Frank Chartes DeRalph, a music professor in New York City. He trained opera singers during the summer at his home. This building was razed in the early 1960s. (Courtesy of Gene and Carol Husson.)

This is a 1926 photograph of the Husson Homestead known as the "Sunshine Cottage" on Twin Lakes Road. DeRalph's Opera Academy once stood adjacent to this home. (Courtesy of Gene and Carol Husson.)

This is a tranquil picture of lower Broad and Water Streets in Milford with the Wright Bridge in the distance. (Courtesy of Kitty Myer.)

Milford, Pa., from the Knobb

Seen here is a 1909 postcard view of Milford and the Delaware River from the Knob. This has always been a favorite spot from which to view our beautiful river valley. (Courtesy of the Hinkel family.)

Known as the "Brick Cottage," this beautiful gothic revival on East Catherine Street was built by Louis Fauchere. It was used as a guesthouse for Hotel Fauchere visitors, *c*. 1895. It is now owned by Diane A. Winecoff. (Collection of the Pike County Historical Society.)

This is a picture of the Ryder Homestead on Water Street in Milford. The image was taken in the 1920s. This building presently houses the Gerola Art Gallery. (Courtesy of Donald Gerola.)

Known as "The Columns" since its construction in the early 1900s, this stately home belonged to the Edward McLaughlin family and was used as a summer residence. This aerial photograph from 1935 shows its beautiful landscaped property. Today The Columns houses the Pike County Historical Society, home of the bloodstained flag that was laid under the head of Pres. Abraham Lincoln as he lay dying. (Collection of the Pike County Historical Society.)

This rare 1889 photograph shows the "Emily Cottage" on the corner of Sixth and West Ann Streets in Milford. The home was built in 1850 as the first "Presbyterian Parsonage." This interesting building has gone through many distinct architectural changes and today is hardly recognizable as the same building. Today it is the home of Valerie Meyer. (Courtesy of Wendy Steuber.)

This author believes this 1889 photograph is the Hankins Farmhouse on the Old Milford Road in Milford Township. The reason for this belief is that the stars carved on the brackets match those that can be seen on this home. Today many historic homes have ornamental brackets, but none could be found with this design. The man and woman seated in the forefront of this photograph are also shown in the Emily Cottage picture. Although I asked many people, no one in this area was able to identify these individuals. This is why it is so important to label and date photographs, because today's pictures become tomorrow's history and it is vital to preserve what occurred in bygone days. (Courtesy of Wendy Steuber.)